The Fatal Boots

William Makepeace Thackeray

Contents

JANUARY.--THE BIRTH OF THE YEAR. 7
FEBRUARY.--CUTTING WEATHER. 11
MARCH.--SHOWERY. 15
APRIL.--FOOLING 19
MAY.--RESTORATION DAY. 23
JUNE.--MARROWBONES AND CLEAVERS. 28
JULY.--SUMMARY PROCEEDINGS. 32
AUGUST.--DOGS HAVE THEIR DAYS. 36
SEPTEMBER.--PLUCKING A GOOSE. 40
OCTOBER.--MARS AND VENUS IN OPPOSITION. 44
NOVEMBER.--A GENERAL POST DELIVERY. 48
DECEMBER.--"THE WINTER OF OUR DISCONTENT." 52

THE FATAL BOOTS

BY

William Makepeace Thackeray

JANUARY.--THE BIRTH OF THE YEAR.

Some poet has observed, that if any man would write down what has really happened to him in this mortal life, he would be sure to make a good book, though he never had met with a single adventure from his birth to his burial. How much more, then, must I, who HAVE had adventures, most singular, pathetic, and unparalleled, be able to compile an instructive and entertaining volume for the use of the public.

I don't mean to say that I have killed lions, or seen the wonders of travel in the deserts of Arabia or Prussia; or that I have been a very fashionable character, living with dukes and peeresses, and writing my recollections of them, as the way now is. I never left this my native isle, nor spoke to a lord (except an Irish one, who had rooms in our house, and forgot to pay three weeks' lodging and extras); but, as our immortal bard observes, I have in the course of my existence been so eaten up by the slugs and harrows of outrageous fortune, and have been the object of such continual and extraordinary ill-luck, that I believe it would melt the heart of a milestone to read of it--that is, if a milestone had a heart of anything but stone.

Twelve of my adventures, suitable for meditation and perusal during the twelve months of the year, have been arranged by me for this work. They contain a part of the history of a great, and, confidently I may say, a GOOD man. I was not a spendthrift like other men. I never wronged any man of a shilling, though I am as sharp a fellow at a bargain as any in Europe. I never injured a fellow-creature; on the contrary, on several occasions, when injured myself, have shown the most wonderful forbearance. I come of a tolerably good family; and yet, born to wealth--of an inoffensive disposition, careful of the money that I had, and eager to get more,--I have been going down hill ever since my journey of life began, and have been pursued by a complication of misfortunes such as surely never happened to any man but the unhappy Bob Stubbs.

Bob Stubbs is my name; and I haven't got a shilling: I have borne the commission of lieutenant in the service of King George, and am NOW--but never mind what I am now, for the public will know in a few pages more. My father was of the Suffolk Stubbses--a well-to-do gentleman of Bungay. My grandfather had been a respected attorney in that town, and left my papa a pretty little fortune. I was thus the inheritor of competence, and ought to be at this moment a gentleman.

My misfortunes may be said to have commenced about a year before my birth, when my papa, a young fellow pretending to study the law in London, fell madly in love with Miss Smith, the daughter of a tradesman, who did not give her a sixpence, and afterwards became bankrupt. My papa married this Miss Smith, and carried her off to the country, where I was born, in an evil hour for me.

Were I to attempt to describe my early years, you would laugh at me as an impostor; but the following letter from mamma to a friend, after her marriage, will pretty well show you what a poor foolish creature she was; and what a reckless extravagant fellow was my other unfortunate parent:--

"TO MISS ELIZA KICKS, IN GRACECHURCH STREET, LONDON.

"OH, ELIZA! your Susan is the happiest girl under heaven! My Thomas is an angel! not a tall grenadier-like looking fellow, such as I always vowed I would marry:--on the contrary, he is what the world would call dumpy, and I hesitate not to confess, that his eyes have a cast in them. But what then? when one of his eyes is fixed on me, and one on my babe, they are lighted up with an affection which my pen cannot describe, and which, certainly, was never bestowed upon any woman so strongly as upon your happy Susan Stubbs.

"When he comes home from shooting, or the farm, if you COULD see dear Thomas with me and our dear little Bob! as I sit on one knee, and baby on the other, and as he dances us both about. I often wish that we had Sir Joshua, or some great painter, to depict the group; for sure it is the prettiest picture in the whole world, to see three such loving merry people.

"Dear baby is the most lovely little creature that CAN POSSIBLY BE,--the very IMAGE of papa; he is cutting his teeth, and the delight of EVERYBODY. Nurse says that, when he is older he will get rid of his squint, and his hair will get a GREAT DEAL less red. Doctor Bates is as kind, and skilful, and attentive as we could desire.

Think what a blessing to have had him! Ever since poor baby's birth, it has never had a day of quiet; and he has been obliged to give it from three to four doses every week;--how thankful ought we to be that the DEAR THING is as well as it is! It got through the measles wonderfully; then it had a little rash; and then a nasty hooping-cough; and then a fever, and continual pains in its poor little stomach, crying, poor dear child, from morning till night.

"But dear Tom is an excellent nurse; and many and many a night has he had no sleep, dear man! in consequence of the poor little baby. He walks up and down with it FOR HOURS, singing a kind of song (dear fellow, he has no more voice than a tea-kettle), and bobbing his head backwards and forwards, and looking, in his nightcap and dressing-gown, SO DROLL. Oh, Eliza! how you would laugh to see him.

"We have one of the best nursemaids IN THE WORLD,--an Irishwoman, who is as fond of baby almost as his mother (but that can NEVER BE). She takes it to walk in the park for hours together, and I really don't know why Thomas dislikes her. He says she is tipsy, very often, and slovenly, which I cannot conceive;--to be sure, the nurse is sadly dirty, and sometimes smells very strong of gin.

"But what of that?--these little drawbacks only make home more pleasant. When one thinks how many mothers have NO nursemaids: how many poor dear children have no doctors: ought we not to be thankful for Mary Malowney, and that Dr. Bates's bill is forty-seven pounds? How ill must dear baby have been, to require so much physic!

"But they are a sad expense, these dear babies, after all. Fancy, Eliza, how much this Mary Malowney costs us. Ten shillings every week; a glass of brandy or gin at dinner; three pint-bottles of Mr. Thrale's best porter every day,--making twenty-one in a week, and nine hundred and ninety in the eleven months she has been with us. Then, for baby, there is Dr. Bates's bill of forty-five guineas, two guineas for christening, twenty for a grand christening supper and ball (rich uncle John mortally offended because he was made godfather, and had to give baby a silver cup: he has struck Thomas out of his will: and old Mr. Firkin quite as much hurt because he was NOT asked: he will not speak to me or Thomas in consequence) twenty guineas for flannels, laces, little gowns, caps, napkins, and such baby's ware: and all this out of 300L. a year! But Thomas expects to make A GREAT DEAL by his farm.

"We have got the most charming country-house YOU CAN IMAGINE: it is QUITE SHUT IN by trees, and so retired that, though only thirty miles from London, the post comes to us but once a week. The roads, it must be confessed, are execrable; it is winter now, and we are up to our knees in mud and snow. But oh, Eliza! how happy we are: with Thomas (he has had a sad attack of rheumatism, dear man!) and little Bobby, and our kind friend Dr. Bates, who comes so far to see us, I leave you to fancy that we have a charming merry party, and do not care for all the gayeties of Ranelagh.

"Adieu! dear baby is crying for his mamma. A thousand kisses from your affectionate

"SUSAN STUBBS."

There it is! Doctor's bills, gentleman-farming, twenty-one pints of porter a week. In this way my unnatural parents were already robbing me of my property.

FEBRUARY.--CUTTING WEATHER.

I have called this chapter "cutting weather," partly in compliment to the month of February, and partly in respect of my own misfortunes, which you are going to read about. For I have often thought that January (which is mostly twelfth-cake and holiday time) is like the first four or five years of a little boy's life; then comes dismal February, and the working-days with it, when chaps begin to look out for themselves, after the Christmas and the New Year's heyday and merrymaking are over, which our infancy may well be said to be. Well can I recollect that bitter first of February, when I first launched out into the world and appeared at Doctor Swishtail's academy.

I began at school that life of prudence and economy which I have carried on ever since. My mother gave me eighteenpence on setting out (poor soul! I thought her heart would break as she kissed me, and bade God bless me); and, besides, I had a small capital of my own which I had amassed for a year previous. I'll tell you, what I used to do. Wherever I saw six halfpence I took one. If it was asked for I said I had taken it and gave it back;--if it was not missed, I said nothing about it, as why should I?--those who don't miss their money, don't lose their money. So I had a little private fortune of three shillings, besides mother's eighteenpence. At school they called me the copper-merchant, I had such lots of it.

Now, even at a preparatory school, a well-regulated boy may better himself: and I can tell you I did. I never was in any quarrels: I never was very high in the class or very low: but there was no chap so much respected:--and why? I'D ALWAYS MONEY. The other boys spent all theirs in the first day or two, and they gave me plenty of cakes and barley-sugar then, I can tell you. I'd no need to spend my own money, for they would insist upon treating me. Well, in a week, when theirs was gone, and they had but their threepence a week to look to for the rest of the half-year, what did I do? Why, I am proud to say that three-halfpence out of the threepence a week of almost all the young gentlemen at Dr. Swishtail's, came into my pocket. Suppose, for instance, Tom Hicks wanted a slice of gingerbread, who had the money? Little Bob Stubbs, to be sure. "Hicks," I used to say, "I'LL buy you three halfp'orth of gingerbread, if you'll give me threepence next Saturday." And he agreed; and next Saturday came, and he very often could not pay me more than three-halfpence. Then there was the threepence I was to have THE NEXT Saturday. I'll tell you what I did for a whole half-year:--I lent a chap, by the name of Dick Bunting, three-halfpence the first Saturday for three-pence the next: he could not pay me more than half when Saturday came, and I'm blest if I did not make him pay me three-halfpence FOR THREE-AND-TWENTY WEEKS RUNNING, making two shillings and tenpence-halfpenny. But he was a sad dishonorable fellow, Dick Bunting; for after I'd been so kind to him, and let him off for three-and-twenty-weeks the money he owed me, holidays came, and threepence he owed me still. Well, according to the common principles of practice, after six-weeks' holidays, he ought to have paid me exactly sixteen shillings, which was my due. For the

First week the 3d. would be	6d.	Fourth week	4s.
Second week	1s.	Fifth week	8s.
Third week	2s.	Sixth week	16s.

Nothing could be more just; and yet--will it be believed? when Bunting came back he offered me THREE-HALFPENCE! the mean, dishonest scoundrel.

However, I was even with him, I can tell you.--He spent all his money in a fortnight, and THEN I screwed him down! I made him, besides giving me a penny for a penny, pay me a quarter of his bread and butter at breakfast and a quarter of his cheese at supper; and before the half-year was out, I got from him a silver fruit-knife, a box of compasses, and a very pretty silver-laced waistcoat, in which I went home as proud as a king: and, what's more, I had no less than three golden guineas in the pocket of it, besides fifteen shillings, the knife, and a brass bottle-screw, which I got from another chap. It wasn't bad interest for twelve shillings--which was all the money I'd had in the year--was it? Heigho! I've often wished that I could get such a chance again in this wicked world; but men are more avaricious now than they used to be in those dear early days.

Well, I went home in my new waistcoat as fine as a peacock; and when I gave the bottle-screw to my father, begging him to take it as a token of my affection for him, my dear mother burst into such a fit of tears as I never saw, and kissed and hugged me fit to smother me. "Bless him, bless him," says she, "to think of his old father. And where did you purchase it, Bob?"--"Why, mother," says I, "I purchased it out of my savings" (which was as true as the gospel).--When I said this, mother looked round to father, smiling, although she had tears in her eyes, and she took his hand, and with her other hand drew me to her. "Is he not a noble boy?" says she to my father: "and only nine years old!"--"Faith," says my father, "he IS a good lad, Susan. Thank thee, my boy: and here is a crown-piece in return for thy bottle-screw--it shall open us a bottle of the very best too," says my father. And he kept his word. I always was fond of good wine (though never, from a motive of proper self-denial, having any in my cellar); and, by Jupiter! on this night I had my little skinful,--for there was no stinting,--so pleased were my dear parents with the bottle-screw. The best of it was, it only cost me threepence originally, which a chap could not pay me.

Seeing this game was such a good one, I became very generous towards my parents; and a capital way it is to encourage liberality in children. I gave mamma a very neat brass thimble, and she gave me a half-guinea piece. Then I gave her a very pretty needle-book, which I made myself with an ace of spades from a new pack of cards we had, and I got Sally, our maid, to cover it with a bit of pink satin her mistress had given her; and I made the leaves of the book, which I vandyked very nicely, out of a piece of flannel I had had round my neck for a sore throat. It smelt a little of hartshorn, but it was a beautiful needle-book; and mamma was so delighted with it, that she went into town and bought me a gold-laced hat. Then I bought papa a pretty china tobacco-stopper: but I am sorry to say of my dear father that he was not so generous as my mamma or myself, for he only burst out laughing, and did not give me so much as a half-crown piece, which was the least I expected from him. "I shan't give you anything, Bob, this time," says he; "and I wish, my boy, you would not make any more such presents,--for, really, they are too expensive." Expensive indeed! I hate meanness,--even in a father.

I must tell you about the silver-edged waistcoat which Bunting gave me. Mamma asked me about it, and I told her the truth,--that it was a present from one of the boys for my kindness to him. Well, what does she do but writes back to Dr. Swishtail, when I went to school, thanking him for his attention to her dear son, and sending a shilling to the good and grateful little boy who had given me the waistcoat!

"What waistcoat is it," says the Doctor to me, "and who gave it to you?"

"Bunting gave it me, sir," says I.

"Call Bunting!" and up the little ungrateful chap came. Would you believe it, he burst into tears,--told that the waistcoat had been given him by his mother, and that he had been forced to give it for a debt to Copper-Merchant, as the nasty little blackguard called me? He then said how, for three-halfpence, he had been compelled to pay me three shillings (the sneak! as if he had been OBLIGED to borrow the three-halfpence!)--how all the other boys had been swindled (swindled!) by me in like manner,--and how, with only twelve shillings, I had managed to scrape together four guineas. . . . .

My courage almost fails me as I describe the shameful scene that followed. The boys were called in, my own little account-book was dragged out of my cupboard, to prove how much I had received from each, and every farthing of my money was paid back to them. The tyrant took the thirty shillings that my dear parents had given me, and said he should put them into the poor-box at church; and, after having made a long discourse to the boys about meanness and usury, he said, "Take off your coat, Mr. Stubbs, and restore Bunting his waistcoat." I did, and stood without coat and waistcoat in the midst of the nasty grinning boys. I was going to put on my coat,--

"Stop!" says he. "TAKE DOWN HIS BREECHES!"

Ruthless, brutal villain! Sam Hopkins, the biggest boy, took them down--horsed me--and I WAS FLOGGED, SIR: yes, flogged! O revenge! I, Robert Stubbs, who had done nothing but what was right, was brutally flogged at ten years of age!--Though February was the shortest month, I remembered it long.

MARCH.--SHOWERY.

When my mamma heard of the treatment of her darling she was for bringing an action against the schoolmaster, or else for tearing his eyes out (when, dear soul! she would not have torn the eyes out of a flea, had it been her own injury), and, at the very least, for having me removed from the school where I had been so shamefully treated. But papa was stern for once, and vowed that I had been served quite right, declared that I should not be removed from school, and sent old Swishtail a brace of pheasants for what he called his kindness to me. Of these the old gentleman invited me to partake, and made a very queer speech at dinner, as he was cutting them up, about the excellence of my parents, and his own determination to be KINDER STILL to me, if ever I ventured on such practices again. So I was obliged to give up my old trade of lending: for the Doctor declared that any boy who borrowed should be flogged, and any one who PAID should be flogged twice as much. There was no standing against such a prohibition as this, and my little commerce was ruined.

I was not very high in the school: not having been able to get farther than that dreadful Propria quae maribus in the Latin grammar, of which, though I have it by heart even now, I never could understand a syllable: but, on account of my size, my age, and the prayers of my mother, was allowed to have the privilege of the bigger boys, and on holidays to walk about in the town. Great dandies we were, too, when we thus went out. I recollect my costume very well: a thunder-and-lightning coat, a white waistcoat embroidered neatly at the pockets, a lace frill, a pair of knee-breeches, and elegant white cotton or silk stockings. This did very well, but still I was dissatisfied: I wanted A PAIR OF BOOTS. Three boys in the school had boots--I was mad to have them too.

But my papa, when I wrote to him, would not hear of it; and three pounds, the price of a pair, was too large a sum for my mother to take from the housekeeping, or for me to pay, in the present impoverished state of my exchequer; but the desire for the boots was so strong, that have them I must at any rate.

There was a German bootmaker who had just set up in OUR town in those days, who afterwards made his fortune in London. I determined to have the boots from him, and did not despair, before the end of a year or two, either to leave the school, when I should not mind his dunning me, or to screw the money from mamma, and so pay him.

So I called upon this man--Stiffelkind was his name--and he took my measure for a pair.

"You are a vary yong gentleman to wear dop-boots," said the shoemaker.

"I suppose, fellow," says I, "that is my business and not yours. Either make the boots or not--but when you speak to a man of my rank, speak respectfully!" And I poured out a number of oaths, in order to impress him with a notion of my respectability.

They had the desired effect. "Stay, sir," says he. "I have a nice littel pair of dop-boots dat I tink will jost do for you." And he produced, sure enough, the most elegant things I ever saw. "Day were made," said he, "for de Honorable Mr. Stiffney, of de Gards, but were too small."

"Ah, indeed!" said I. "Stiffney is a relation of mine. And what, you scoundrel, will you have the impudence to ask for these things?" He replied, "Three pounds."

"Well," said I, "they are confoundedly dear; but, as you will have a long time to wait for your money, why, I shall have my revenge you see." The man looked alarmed, and began a speech: "Sare,--I cannot let dem go vidout"--but a bright thought struck me, and I interrupted--"Sir! don't sir me. Take off the boots, fellow, and, hark ye, when you speak to a nobleman, don't say--Sir."

"A hundert tousand pardons, my lort," says he: "if I had known you were a lort, I vood never have called you--Sir. Vat name shall I put down in my books?"

"Name?--oh! why, Lord Cornwallis, to be sure," said I, as I walked off in the boots.

"And vat shall I do vid my lort's shoes?"

"Keep them until I send for them," said I. And, giving him a patronizing bow, I walked out of the shop, as the German tied up my shoes in paper.

*****

    This story I would not have told, but that my whole life turned upon these accursed boots. I walked back to school as proud as a peacock, and easily succeeded in satisfying the boys as to the manner in which I came by my new ornaments.
    Well, one fatal Monday morning--the blackest of all black-Mondays that ever I knew--as we were all of us playing between school-hours, I saw a posse of boys round a stranger, who seemed to be looking out for one of us. A sudden trembling seized me--I knew it was Stiffelkind. What had brought him here? He talked loud, and seemed angry. So I rushed into the school-room, and burying my head between my hands, began reading for dear life.
    "I vant Lort Cornvallis," said the horrid bootmaker. "His lortship belongs, I know, to dis honorable school, for I saw him vid de boys at chorch yesterday."
    "Lord who?"
    "Vy, Lort Cornvallis to be sure--a very fat yong nobeman, vid red hair: he squints a little, and svears dreadfully."
    "There's no Lord Cornvallis here," said one; and there was a pause.
    "Stop! I have it," says that odious Bunting. "IT MUST BE STUBBS!" And "Stubbs! Stubbs!" every one cried out, while I was so busy at my book as not to hear a word.
    At last, two of the biggest chaps rushed into the schoolroom, and seizing each an arm, run me into the playground--bolt up against the shoemaker.
    "Dis is my man. I beg your lortship's pardon," says he, "I have brought your lortship's shoes, vich you left. See, dey have been in dis parcel ever since you vent avay in my boots."
    "Shoes, fellow!" says I. "I never saw your face before!" For I knew there was nothing for it but brazening it out. "Upon the honor of a gentleman!" said I, turning round to the boys. They hesitated; and if the trick had turned in my favor, fifty of them would have seized hold of Stiffelkind and drubbed him soundly.
    "Stop!" says Bunting (hang him!) "Let's see the shoes. If they fit him, why then the cobbler's right." They did fit me; and not only that, but the name of STUBBS

was written in them at full length.

"Vat!" said Stiffelkind. "Is he not a lort? So help me Himmel, I never did vonce tink of looking at de shoes, which have been lying ever since in dis piece of brown paper." And then, gathering anger as he went on, he thundered out so much of his abuse of me, in his German-English, that the boys roared with laughter. Swishtail came in in the midst of the disturbance, and asked what the noise meant.

"It's only Lord Cornwallis, sir," said the boys, "battling with his shoemaker about the price of a pair of top-boots."

"Oh, sir," said I, "it was only in fun that I called myself Lord Cornwallis."

"In fun!--Where are the boots? And you, sir, give me your bill." My beautiful boots were brought; and Stiffelkind produced his bill. "Lord Cornwallis to Samuel Stiffelkind, for a pair of boots--four guineas."

"You have been fool enough, sir," says the Doctor, looking very stern, "to let this boy impose on you as a lord; and knave enough to charge him double the value of the article you sold him. Take back the boots, sir! I won't pay a penny of your bill; nor can you get a penny. As for you, sir, you miserable swindler and cheat, I shall not flog you as I did before, but I shall send you home: you are not fit to be the companion of honest boys."

"SUPPOSE WE DUCK HIM before he goes?" piped out a very small voice. The Doctor grinned significantly, and left the school-room; and the boys knew by this they might have their will. They seized me and carried me to the playground pump: they pumped upon me until I was half dead; and the monster, Stiffelkind, stood looking on for the half-hour the operation lasted.

I suppose the Doctor, at last, thought I had had pumping enough, for he rang the school-bell, and the boys were obliged to leave me. As I got out of the trough, Stiffelkind was alone with me. "Vell, my lort," says he, "you have paid SOME-THING for dese boots, but not all. By Jubider, YOU SHALL NEVER HEAR DE END OF DEM." And I didn't.

APRIL.--FOOLING.

After this, as you may fancy, I left this disgusting establishment, and lived for some time along with pa and mamma at home. My education was finished, at least mamma and I agreed that it was; and from boyhood until hobbadyhoyhood (which I take to be about the sixteenth year of the life of a young man, and may be likened to the month of April when spring begins to bloom)--from fourteen until seventeen, I say, I remained at home, doing nothing--for which I have ever since had a great taste--the idol of my mamma, who took part in all my quarrels with father, and used regularly to rob the weekly expenses in order to find me in pocket-money. Poor soul! many and many is the guinea I have had from her in that way; and so she enabled me to cut a very pretty figure.

Papa was for having me at this time articled to a merchant, or put to some profession; but mamma and I agreed that I was born to be a gentleman and not a tradesman, and the army was the only place for me. Everybody was a soldier in those times, for the French war had just begun, and the whole country was swarming with militia regiments. "We'll get him a commission in a marching regiment," said my father. "As we have no money to purchase him up, he'll FIGHT his way, I make no doubt." And papa looked at me with a kind of air of contempt, as much as to say he doubted whether I should be very eager for such a dangerous way of bettering myself.

I wish you could have heard mamma's screech when he talked so coolly of my going out to fight! "What! send him abroad, across the horrid, horrid sea--to be wrecked and perhaps drowned, and only to land for the purpose of fighting the wicked Frenchmen,--to be wounded, and perhaps kick--kick--killed! Oh, Thomas, Thomas! would you murder me and your boy?" There was a regular scene. However, it ended--as it always did--in mother's getting the better, and it was settled that I should go into the militia. And why not? The uniform is just as handsome, and the danger not half so great. I don't think in the course of my whole military experience I ever fought anything, except an old woman, who had the impudence to hallo out, "Heads up, lobster!"--Well, I joined the North Bungays, and was fairly launched into the world.

I was not a handsome man, I know; but there was SOMETHING about me--that's very evident--for the girls always laughed when they talked to me, and the men, though they affected to call me a poor little creature, squint-eyes, knock-knees, redhead, and so on, were evidently annoyed by my success, for they hated me so confoundedly. Even at the present time they go on, though I have given up gallivanting, as I call it. But in the April of my existence,--that is, in anno Domini 1791, or so--it was a different case; and having nothing else to do, and being bent upon bettering my condition, I did some very pretty things in that way. But I was not hot-headed and imprudent, like most young fellows. Don't fancy I looked for beauty! Pish!--I wasn't such a fool. Nor for temper; I don't care about a bad temper: I could break any woman's heart in two years. What I wanted was to get on in the world. Of course I didn't PREFER an ugly woman, or a shrew; and when the choice offered, would certainly put up with a handsome, good-humored girl, with plenty of money, as any honest man would.

Now there were two tolerably rich girls in our parts: Miss Magdalen Crutty, with twelve thousand pounds (and, to do her justice, as plain a girl as ever I saw), and Miss Mary Waters, a fine, tall, plump, smiling, peach-cheeked, golden-haired, white-skinned lass, with only ten. Mary Waters lived with her uncle, the Doctor, who had helped me into the world, and who was trusted with this little orphan charge very soon after. My mother, as you have heard, was so fond of Bates, and Bates so fond of little Mary, that both, at first, were almost always in our house; and I used to call her my little wife as soon as I could speak, and before she could walk almost. It was beautiful to see us, the neighbors said.

Well, when her brother, the lieutenant of an India ship, came to be captain, and actually gave Mary five thousand pounds, when she was about ten years old, and promised her five thousand more, there was a great talking, and bobbing, and smiling between the Doctor and my parents, and Mary and I were left together more than ever, and she was told to call me her little husband. And she did; and it was considered a settled thing from that day. She was really amazingly fond of me.

Can any one call me mercenary after that? Though Miss Crutty had twelve thousand, and Mary only ten (five in hand, and five in the bush), I stuck faithfully to Mary. As a matter of course, Miss Crutty hated Miss Waters. The fact was, Mary had all the country dangling after her, and not a soul would come to Magdalen, for all her 12,000L. I used to be attentive to her though (as it's always useful to be); and Mary would sometimes laugh and sometimes cry at my flirting with Magdalen. This I thought proper very quickly to check. "Mary," said I, "you know that my love for you is disinterested,--for I am faithful to you, though Miss Crutty is richer than you. Don't fly into a rage, then, because I pay her attentions, when you know that my heart and my promise are engaged to you."

The fact is, to tell a little bit of a secret, there is nothing like the having two strings to your bow. "Who knows?" thought I. "Mary may die; and then where are my 10,000L.?" So I used to be very kind indeed to Miss Crutty; and well it was that I was so: for when I was twenty and Mary eighteen, I'm blest if news did not arrive that Captain Waters, who was coming home to England with all his money in rupees, had been taken--ship, rupees, self and all--by a French privateer; and Mary, instead of 10,000L. had only 5,000L., making a difference of no less than 350L. per annum betwixt her and Miss Crutty.

I had just joined my regiment (the famous North Bungay Fencibles, Colonel Craw commanding) when this news reached me; and you may fancy how a young man, in an expensive regiment and mess, having uniforms and what not to pay for, and a figure to cut in the world, felt at hearing such news! "My dearest Robert," wrote Miss Waters, "will deplore my dear brother's loss: but not, I am sure, the money which that kind and generous soul had promised me. I have still five thousand pounds, and with this and your own little fortune (I had 1,000L. in the Five per Cents!) we shall be as happy and contented as possible."

Happy and contented indeed! Didn't I know how my father got on with his 300L. a year, and how it was all he could do out of it to add a hundred a year to my narrow income, and live himself! My mind was made up. I instantly mounted the coach and flew to our village,--to Mr. Crutty's, of course. It was next door to Doctor Bates's; but I had no business THERE.

I found Magdalen in the garden. "Heavens, Mr. Stubbs!" said she, as in my new uniform I appeared before her, "I really did never--such a handsome officer--expect to see you." And she made as if she would blush, and began to tremble violently. I led her to a garden-seat. I seized her hand--it was not withdrawn. I pressed it;--I thought the pressure was returned. I flung myself on my knees, and then I poured into her ear a little speech which I had made on the top of the coach. "Divine Miss Crutty," said I; "idol of my soul! It was but to catch one glimpse of you that I passed through this garden. I never intended to breathe the secret passion" (oh, no; of course not) "which was wearing my life away. You know my unfortunate pre-engagement--it is broken, and FOR EVER! I am free;--free, but to be your slave,--your humblest, fondest, truest slave!" And so on. . . . .

"Oh, Mr. Stubbs," said she, as I imprinted a kiss upon her cheek, "I can't refuse you; but I fear you are a sad naughty man. . . . ."

Absorbed in the delicious reverie which was caused by the dear creature's confusion, we were both silent for a while, and should have remained so for hours perhaps, so lost were we in happiness, had I not been suddenly roused by a voice exclaiming from behind us--

"DON'T CRY, MARY! HE IS A SWINDLING, SNEAKING SCOUNDREL, AND YOU ARE WELL RID OF HIM!"

I turned round. O heaven, there stood Mary, weeping on Doctor Bates's arm, while that miserable apothecary was looking at me with the utmost scorn. The gardener, who had let me in, had told them of my arrival, and now stood grinning behind them. "Imperence!" was my Magdalen's only exclamation, as she flounced by with the utmost self-possession, while I, glancing daggers at the SPIES, followed her. We retired to the parlor, where she repeated to me the strongest assurances of her love.

I thought I was a made man. Alas! I was only an APRIL FOOL!

MAY.--RESTORATION DAY.

As the month of May is considered, by poets and other philosophers, to be devoted by Nature to the great purpose of love-making, I may as well take advantage of that season and acquaint you with the result of MY amours.

Young, gay, fascinating, and an ensign--I had completely won the heart of my Magdalen; and as for Miss Waters and her nasty uncle the Doctor, there was a complete split between us, as you may fancy; Miss pretending, forsooth, that she was glad I had broken off the match, though she would have given her eyes, the little minx, to have had it on again. But this was out of the question. My father, who had all sorts of queer notions, said I had acted like a rascal in the business; my mother took my part, in course, and declared I acted rightly, as I always did: and I got leave of absence from the regiment in order to press my beloved Magdalen to marry me out of hand--knowing, from reading and experience, the extraordinary mutability of human affairs.

Besides, as the dear girl was seventeen years older than myself, and as bad in health as she was in temper, how was I to know that the grim king of terrors might not carry her off before she became mine? With the tenderest warmth, then, and most delicate ardor, I continued to press my suit. The happy day was fixed--the ever memorable 10th of May, 1792. The wedding-clothes were ordered; and, to make things secure, I penned a little paragraph for the county paper to this effect:--"Marriage in High Life. We understand that Ensign Stubbs, of the North Bungay Fencibles, and son of Thomas Stubbs, of Sloffemsquiggle, Esquire, is about to lead to the hymeneal altar the lovely and accomplished daughter of Solomon Crutty, Esquire, of the same place. A fortune of twenty thousand pounds is, we hear, the lady's portion. 'None but the brave deserve the fair.'"

*****

"Have you informed your relatives, my beloved?" said I to Magdalen, one day after sending the above notice; "will any of them attend at your marriage?"

"Uncle Sam will, I dare say," said Miss Crutty, "dear mamma's brother."

"And who WAS your dear mamma?" said I: for Miss Crutty's respected parent had been long since dead, and I never heard her name mentioned in the family.

Magdalen blushed, and cast down her eyes to the ground. "Mamma was a foreigner," at last she said.

"And of what country?"

"A German. Papa married her when she was very young:--she was not of a very good family," said Miss Crutty, hesitating.

"And what care I for family, my love!" said I, tenderly kissing the knuckles of the hand which I held. "She must have been an angel who gave birth to you."

"She was a shoemaker's daughter."

"A GERMAN SHOEMAKER! Hang 'em," thought I, "I have had enough of them;" and so broke up this conversation, which did not somehow please me.

*****

Well, the day was drawing near: the clothes were ordered; the banns were read. My dear mamma had built a cake about the size of a washing-tub; and I was only waiting for a week to pass to put me in possession of twelve thousand pounds in the FIVE per Cents, as they were in those days, heaven bless 'em! Little did I know the storm that was brewing, and the disappointment which was to fall upon a young man who really did his best to get a fortune.

*****

"Oh, Robert," said my Magdalen to me, two days before the match was to come off, "I have SUCH a kind letter from uncle Sam in London. I wrote to him as you wished. He says that he is coming down to-morrow, that he has heard of you often, and knows your character very well; and that he has got a VERY HANDSOME PRESENT for us! What can it be, I wonder?"

"Is he rich, my soul's adored?" says I.

"He is a bachelor, with a fine trade, and nobody to leave his money to."

"His present can't be less than a thousand pounds?" says I.

"Or, perhaps, a silver tea-set, and some corner-dishes," says she.

But we could not agree to this: it was too little--too mean for a man of her uncle's wealth; and we both determined it must be the thousand pounds.

"Dear good uncle! he's to be here by the coach," says Magdalen. "Let us ask a little party to meet him." And so we did, and so they came: my father and mother, old Crutty in his best wig, and the parson who was to marry us the next day. The coach was to come in at six. And there was the tea-table, and there was the punch-bowl, and everybody ready and smiling to receive our dear uncle from London.

Six o'clock came, and the coach, and the man from the "Green Dragon" with a portmanteau, and a fat old gentleman walking behind, of whom I just caught a glimpse--a venerable old gentleman: I thought I'd seen him before.

*****

Then there was a ring at the bell; then a scuffling and bumping in the passage: then old Crutty rushed out, and a great laughing and talking, and "HOW ARE YOU?" and so on, was heard at the door; and then the parlor-door was flung open, and Crutty cried out with a loud voice--

"Good people all! my brother-in-law, Mr. STIFFELKIND!"

MR. STIFFELKIND!--I trembled as I heard the name!

Miss Crutty kissed him; mamma made him a curtsy, and papa made him a bow; and Dr. Snorter, the parson, seized his hand and shook it most warmly: then came my turn!

"Vat!" says he. "It is my dear goot yong frend from Doctor Schvis'hentail's! is dis de yong gentleman's honorable moder" (mamma smiled and made a curtsy), "and dis his fader? Sare and madam, you should be broud of soch a sonn. And you my niece, if you have him for a husband you vill be locky, dat is all. Vat dink you, broder Croty, and Madame Stobbs, I 'ave made your sonn's boots! Ha--ha!"

My mamma laughed, and said, "I did not know it, but I am sure, sir, he has as pretty a leg for a boot as any in the whole county."

Old Stiffelkind roared louder. "A very nice leg, ma'am, and a very SHEAP BOOT TOO. Vat! did you not know I make his boots? Perhaps you did not know something else too--p'raps you did not know" (and here the monster clapped his hand on the table and made the punch-ladle tremble in the bowl)--"p'raps you did not know as dat yong man, dat Stobbs, dat sneaking, baltry, squinting fellow, is as vicked as he is ogly. He bot a pair of boots from me and never paid for dem. Dat is noting, nobody never pays; but he bought a pair of boots, and called himself Lord Cornvallis. And I was fool enough to believe him vonce. But look you, niece Magdalen, I 'ave got five tousand pounds: if you marry him I vill not give you a benny. But look you what I will gif you: I bromised you a bresent, and I will give you DESE!"

And the old monster produced THOSE VERY BOOTS which Swishtail had made him take back.

*****

I DIDN'T marry Miss Crutty: I am not sorry for it though. She was a nasty, ugly, ill-tempered wretch, and I've always said so ever since.

And all this arose from those infernal boots, and that unlucky paragraph in the county paper--I'll tell you how.

In the first place, it was taken up as a quiz by one of the wicked, profligate, unprincipled organs of the London press, who chose to be very facetious about the "Marriage in High Life," and made all sorts of jokes about me and my dear Miss

Crutty.

Secondly, it was read in this London paper by my mortal enemy, Bunting, who had been introduced to old Stiffelkind's acquaintance by my adventure with him, and had his shoes made regularly by that foreign upstart.

Thirdly, he happened to want a pair of shoes mended at this particular period, and as he was measured by the disgusting old High-Dutch cobbler, he told him his old friend Stubbs was going to be married.

"And to whom?" said old Stiffelkind. "To a voman wit geld, I vill take my oath."

"Yes," says Bunting, "a country girl--a Miss Magdalen Carotty or Crotty, at a place called Sloffemsquiggle."

"SHLOFFEMSCHWIEGEL!" bursts out the dreadful bootmaker. "Mein Gott, mein Gott! das geht nicht! I tell you, sare, it is no go. Miss Crotty is my niece. I vill go down myself. I vill never let her marry dat goot-for-nothing schwindler and tief." SUCH was the language that the scoundrel ventured to use regarding me!

JUNE.--MARROWBONES AND CLEAVERS.

Was there ever such confounded ill-luck? My whole life has been a tissue of ill-luck: although I have labored perhaps harder than any man to make a fortune, something always tumbled it down. In love and in war I was not like others. In my marriages, I had an eye to the main chance; and you see how some unlucky blow would come and throw them over. In the army I was just as prudent, and just as unfortunate. What with judicious betting, and horse-swapping, good-luck at billiards, and economy, I do believe I put by my pay every year,--and that is what few can say who have but an allowance of a hundred a year.

I'll tell you how it was. I used to be very kind to the young men; I chose their horses for them, and their wine: and showed them how to play billiards, or ecarte, of long mornings, when there was nothing better to do. I didn't cheat: I'd rather die than cheat;--but if fellows WILL play, I wasn't the man to say no--why should I? There was one young chap in our regiment of whom I really think I cleared 300L. a year.

His name was Dobble. He was a tailor's son, and wanted to be a gentleman. A poor weak young creature; easy to be made tipsy; easy to be cheated; and easy to be frightened. It was a blessing for him that I found him; for if anybody else had, they would have plucked him of every shilling.

Ensign Dobble and I were sworn friends. I rode his horses for him, and chose his champagne, and did everything, in fact, that a superior mind does for an inferior,--when the inferior has got the money. We were inseparables,--hunting everywhere in couples. We even managed to fall in love with two sisters, as young soldiers will do, you know; for the dogs fall in love, with every change of quarters.

Well, once, in the year 1793 (it was just when the French had chopped poor

Louis's head off), Dobble and I, gay young chaps as ever wore sword by side, had cast our eyes upon two young ladies by the name of Brisket, daughters of a butcher in the town where we were quartered. The dear girls fell in love with us, of course. And many a pleasant walk in the country, many a treat to a tea-garden, many a smart ribbon and brooch used Dobble and I (for his father allowed him 600L., and our purses were in common) present to these young ladies. One day, fancy our pleasure at receiving a note couched thus:--

"DEER CAPTING STUBBS AND DOBBLE--Miss Briskets presents their compliments, and as it is probble that our papa will be till twelve at the corprayshun dinner, we request the pleasure of their company to tea."

Didn't we go! Punctually at six we were in the little back-parlor; we quaffed more Bohea, and made more love, than half a dozen ordinary men could. At nine, a little punch-bowl succeeded to the little teapot; and, bless the girls! a nice fresh steak was frizzling on the gridiron for our supper. Butchers were butchers then, and their parlor was their kitchen too; at least old Brisket's was--one door leading into the shop, and one into the yard, on the other side of which was the slaughter-house.

Fancy, then, our horror when, just at this critical time, we heard the shop-door open, a heavy staggering step on the flags, and a loud husky voice from the shop, shouting, "Hallo, Susan; hallo, Betsy! show a light!" Dobble turned as white as a sheet; the two girls each as red as a lobster; I alone preserved my presence of mind. "The back-door," says I--"The dog's in the court," say they. "He's not so bad as the man," said I. "Stop!" cries Susan, flinging open the door, and rushing to the fire. "Take THIS and perhaps it will quiet him."

What do you think "THIS" was? I'm blest if it was not the STEAK!

She pushed us out, patted and hushed the dog, and was in again in a minute. The moon was shining on the court, and on the slaughter-house, where there hung the white ghastly-looking carcasses of a couple of sheep; a great gutter ran down the court--a gutter of BLOOD! The dog was devouring his beefsteak (OUR beefsteak) in silence; and we could see through the little window the girls hustling about to pack up the supper-things, and presently the shop-door being opened, old Brisket entering, staggering, angry, and drunk. What's more, we could see, perched on a high stool, and nodding politely, as if to salute old Brisket, the FEATHER OF DOBBLE'S

COCKED HAT! When Dobble saw it, he turned white, and deadly sick; and the poor fellow, in an agony of fright, sunk shivering down upon one of the butcher's cutting-blocks, which was in the yard.

We saw old Brisket look steadily (as steadily as he could) at the confounded, impudent, pert, waggling feather; and then an idea began to dawn upon his mind, that there was a head to the hat; and then he slowly rose up--he was a man of six feet, and fifteen stone--he rose up, put on his apron and sleeves, and TOOK DOWN HIS CLEAVER.

"Betsy," says he, "open the yard door." But the poor girls screamed, and flung on their knees, and begged, and wept, and did their very best to prevent him. "OPEN THE YARD DOOR!" says he, with a thundering loud voice; and the great bull-dog, hearing it, started up and uttered a yell which sent me flying to the other end of the court.--Dobble couldn't move; he was sitting on the block, blubbering like a baby.

The door opened, and out Mr. Brisket came.

"TO HIM, JOWLER!" says he. "KEEP HIM, JOWLER!"--and the horrid dog flew at me, and I flew back into the corner, and drew my sword, determining to sell my life dearly.

"That's it," says Brisket. "Keep him there,--good dog,--good dog! And now, sir," says he, turning round to Dobble, "is this your hat?"

"Yes," says Dobble, fit to choke with fright.

"Well, then," says Brisket, "it's my--(hic)--my painful duty to--(hic)--to tell you, that as I've got your hat, I must have your head;--it's painful, but it must be done. You'd better--(hic)--settle yourself com--comfumarably against that--(hic)--that block, and I'll chop it off before you can say Jack--(hic)--no, I mean Jack Robinson."

Dobble went down on his knees and shrieked out, "I'm an only son, Mr. Brisket! I'll marry her, sir; I will, upon my honor, sir.--Consider my mother, sir; consider my mother."

"That's it, sir," says Brisket, "that's a good--(hic)--a good boy;--just put your head down quietly--and I'll have it off--yes, off--as if you were Louis the Six--the Sixtix--the Siktickleteenth.--I'll chop the other CHAP AFTERWARDS."

When I heard this, I made a sudden bound back, and gave such a cry as any man might who was in such a way. The ferocious Jowler, thinking I was going to escape, flew at my throat; screaming furious, I flung out my arms in a kind of desperation,--and, to my wonder, down fell the dog, dead, and run through the body!

*****

At this moment a posse of people rushed in upon old Brisket,--one of his daughters had had the sense to summon them,--and Dobble's head was saved. And when they saw the dog lying dead at my feet, my ghastly look, my bloody sword, they gave me no small credit for my bravery. "A terrible fellow that Stubbs," said they; and so the mess said, the next day.

I didn't tell them that the dog had committed SUICIDE--why should I? And I didn't say a word about Dobble's cowardice. I said he was a brave fellow, and fought like a tiger; and this prevented HIM from telling tales. I had the dogskin made into a pair of pistol-holsters, and looked so fierce, and got such a name for courage in our regiment, that when we had to meet the regulars, Bob Stubbs was always the man put forward to support the honor of the corps. The women, you know, adore courage; and such was my reputation at this time, that I might have had my pick out of half a dozen, with three, four, or five thousand pounds apiece, who were dying for love of me and my red coat. But I wasn't such a fool. I had been twice on the point of marriage, and twice disappointed; and I vowed by all the Saints to have a wife, and a rich one. Depend upon this, as an infallible maxim to guide you through life: IT'S AS EASY TO GET A RICH WIFE AS A POOR ONE;--the same bait that will hook a fly will hook a salmon.

JULY.--SUMMARY PROCEEDINGS.

Dobble's reputation for courage was not increased by the butcher's-dog adventure; but mine stood very high: little Stubbs was voted the boldest chap of all the bold North Bungays. And though I must confess, what was proved by subsequent circumstances, that nature has NOT endowed me with a large, or even, I may say, an average share of bravery, yet a man is very willing to flatter himself to the contrary; and, after a little time, I got to believe that my killing the dog was an action of undaunted courage, and that I was as gallant as any of the one hundred thousand heroes of our army. I always had a military taste-- it's only the brutal part of the profession, the horrid fighting and blood, that I don't like.

I suppose the regiment was not very brave itself--being only militia; but certain it was, that Stubbs was considered a most terrible fellow, and I swore so much, and looked so fierce, that you would have fancied I had made half a hundred campaigns. I was second in several duels; the umpire in all disputes; and such a crack-shot myself, that fellows were shy of insulting me. As for Dobble, I took him under my protection; and he became so attached to me, that we ate, drank, and rode together every day; his father didn't care for money, so long as his son was in good company--and what so good as that of the celebrated Stubbs? Heigho! I WAS good company in those days, and a brave fellow too, as I should have remained, but for--what I shall tell the public immediately.

It happened, in the fatal year ninety-six, that the brave North Bungays were quartered at Portsmouth, a maritime place, which I need not describe, and which I wish I had never seen. I might have been a General now, or, at least, a rich man.

The red-coats carried everything before them in those days; and I, such a crack character as I was in my regiment, was very well received by the townspeople:

many dinners I had; many tea-parties; many lovely young ladies did I lead down the pleasant country-dances.

Well, although I had had the two former rebuffs in love which I have described, my heart was still young; and the fact was, knowing that a girl with a fortune was my only chance, I made love here as furiously as ever. I shan't describe the lovely creatures on whom I fixed, whilst at Portsmouth. I tried more than--several--and it is a singular fact, which I never have been able to account for, that, successful as I was with ladies of maturer age, by the young ones I was refused regular.

But "faint heart never won fair lady;" and so I went on, and on, until I had got a Miss Clopper, a tolerable rich navy-contractor's daughter, into such a way, that I really don't think she could have refused me. Her brother, Captain Clopper, was in a line regiment, and helped me as much as ever he could: he swore I was such a brave fellow.

As I had received a number of attentions from Clopper, I determined to invite him to dinner; which I could do without any sacrifice of my principle upon this point: for the fact is, Dobble lived at an inn, and as he sent all his bills to his father, I made no scruple to use his table. We dined in the coffee-room, Dobble bringing HIS friend; and so we made a party CARRY, as the French say. Some naval officers were occupied in a similar way at a table next to ours.

Well--I didn't spare the bottle, either for myself or for my friends; and we grew very talkative, and very affectionate as the drinking went on. Each man told stories of his gallantry in the field, or amongst the ladies, as officers will, after dinner. Clopper confided to the company his wish that I should marry his sister, and vowed that he thought me the best fellow in Christendom.

Ensign Dobble assented to this. "But let Miss Clopper beware," says he, "for Stubbs is a sad fellow: he has had I don't know how many liaisons already; and he has been engaged to I don't know how many women."

"Indeed!" says Clopper. "Come, Stubbs, tell us your adventures."

"Psha!" said I, modestly, "there is nothing, indeed, to tell. I have been in love, my dear boy--who has not?--and I have been jilted--who has not?"

Clopper swore he would blow his sister's brains out if ever SHE served me so.

"Tell him about Miss Crutty," said Dobble. "He! he! Stubbs served THAT woman out, anyhow; she didn't jilt HIM. I'll be sworn."

"Really, Dobble, you are too bad, and should not mention names. The fact is, the girl was desperately in love with me, and had money--sixty thousand pounds, upon my reputation. Well, everything was arranged, when who should come down from London but a relation."

"Well, and did he prevent the match?"

"Prevent it--yes, sir, I believe you he did; though not in the sense that YOU mean. He would have given his eyes--ay, and ten thousand pounds more--if I would have accepted the girl, but I would not."

"Why, in the name of goodness?"

"Sir, her uncle was a SHOEMAKER. I never would debase myself by marrying into such a family."

"Of course not," said Dobble; "he couldn't, you know. Well, now--tell him about the other girl, Mary Waters, you know."

"Hush, Dobble, hush! don't you see one of those naval officers has turned round and heard you? My dear Clopper, it was a mere childish bagatelle."

"Well, but let's have it," said Clopper--"let's have it. I won't tell my sister, you know." And he put his hand to his nose and looked monstrous wise.

"Nothing of that sort, Clopper--no, no--'pon honor--little Bob Stubbs is no LIBERTINE; and the story is very simple. You see that my father has a small place, merely a few hundred acres, at Sloffemsquiggle. Isn't it a funny name? Hang it, there's the naval gentleman staring again,"--(I looked terribly fierce as I returned this officer's stare, and continued in a loud careless voice). Well, at this Sloffemsquiggle there lived a girl, a Miss Waters, the niece of some blackguard apothecary in the neighborhood; but my mother took a fancy to the girl, and had her up to the park and petted her. We were both young--and--and--the girl fell in love with me, that's the fact. I was obliged to repel some rather warm advances that she made me; and here, upon my honor as a gentleman, you have all the story about which that silly Dobble makes such a noise."

Just as I finished this sentence. I found myself suddenly taken by the nose, and a voice shouting out,--

"Mr. Stubbs, you are A LIAR AND A SCOUNDREL! Take this, sir,--and this, for daring to meddle with the name of an innocent lady."

I turned round as well as I could--for the ruffian had pulled me out of my chair-

-and beheld a great marine monster, six feet high, who was occupied in beating and kicking me, in the most ungentlemanly manner, on my cheeks, my ribs, and between the tails of my coat. "He is a liar, gentlemen, and a scoundrel! The bootmaker had detected him in swindling, and so his niece refused him. Miss Waters was engaged to him from childhood, and he deserted her for the bootmaker's niece, who was richer."--And then sticking a card between my stock and my coat-collar, in what is called the scruff of my neck, the disgusting brute gave me another blow behind my back, and left the coffee-room with his friends.

Dobble raised me up; and taking the card from my neck, read, CAPTAIN WATERS. Clopper poured me out a glass of water, and said in my ear, "If this is true, you are an infernal scoundrel, Stubbs; and must fight me, after Captain Waters;" and he flounced out of the room.

I had but one course to pursue. I sent the Captain a short and contemptuous note, saying that he was beneath my anger. As for Clopper, I did not condescend to notice his remark but in order to get rid of the troublesome society of these low blackguards, I determined to gratify an inclination I had long entertained, and make a little tour. I applied for leave of absence, and set off THAT VERY NIGHT. I can fancy the disappointment of the brutal Waters, on coming, as he did, the next morning to my quarters and finding me GONE. Ha! ha!

After this adventure I became sick of a military life--at least the life of my own regiment, where the officers, such was their unaccountable meanness and prejudice against me, absolutely refused to see me at mess. Colonel Craw sent me a letter to this effect, which I treated as it deserved.--I never once alluded to it in any way, and have since never spoken a single word to any man in the North Bungays.

AUGUST.--DOGS HAVE THEIR DAYS.

See, now, what life is! I have had ill-luck on ill-luck from that day to this. I have sunk in the world, and, instead of riding my horse and drinking my wine, as a real gentleman should, have hardly enough now to buy a pint of ale; ay, and am very glad when anybody will treat me to one. Why, why was I born to undergo such unmerited misfortunes?

You must know that very soon after my adventure with Miss Crutty, and that cowardly ruffian, Captain Waters (he sailed the day after his insult to me, or I should most certainly have blown his brains out; NOW he is living in England, and is my relation; but, of course, I cut the fellow)--very soon after these painful events another happened, which ended, too, in a sad disappointment. My dear papa died, and, instead of leaving five thousand pounds, as I expected at the very least, left only his estate, which was worth but two. The land and house were left to me; to mamma and my sisters he left, to be sure, a sum of two thousand pounds in the hands of that eminent firm Messrs. Pump, Aldgate and Co., which failed within six months after his demise, and paid in five years about one shilling and ninepence in the pound; which really was all my dear mother and sisters had to live upon.

The poor creatures were quite unused to money matters; and, would you believe it? when the news came of Pump and Aldgate's failure, mamma only smiled, and threw her eyes up to heaven, and said, "Blessed be God, that we have still wherewithal to live. There are tens of thousands in this world, dear children, who would count our poverty riches." And with this she kissed my two sisters, who began to blubber, as girls always will do, and threw their arms round her neck, and then round my neck, until I was half stifled with their embraces, and slobbered all over with their tears.

"Dearest mamma," said I, "I am very glad to see the noble manner in which you bear your loss; and more still to know that you are so rich as to be able to put up with it." The fact was, I really thought the old lady had got a private hoard of her own, as many of them have--a thousand pounds or so in a stocking. Had she put by thirty pounds a year, as well she might, for the thirty years of her marriage, there would have been nine hundred pounds clear, and no mistake. But still I was angry to think that any such paltry concealment had been practised--concealment too of MY money; so I turned on her pretty sharply, and continued my speech. "You say, Ma'am, that you are rich, and that Pump and Aldgate's failure has no effect upon you. I am very happy to hear you say so, Ma'am--very happy that you ARE rich; and I should like to know where your property, my father's property, for you had none of your own,--I should like to know where this money lies--WHERE YOU HAVE CONCEALED IT, Ma'am; and, permit me to say, that when I agreed to board you and my two sisters for eighty pounds a year, I did not know that you had OTHER resources than those mentioned in my blessed father's will."

This I said to her because I hated the meanness of concealment, not because I lost by the bargain of boarding them: for the three poor things did not eat much more than sparrows: and I've often since calculated that I had a clear twenty pounds a year profit out of them.

Mamma and the girls looked quite astonished when I made the speech. "What does he mean?" said Lucy to Eliza.

Mamma repeated the question. "My beloved Robert, what concealment are you talking of?"

"I am talking of concealed property, Ma'am," says I sternly.

"And do you--what--can you--do you really suppose that I have concealed--any of that blessed sa-a-a-aint's prop-op-op-operty?" screams out mamma. "Robert," says she--"Bob, my own darling boy--my fondest, best beloved, now HE is gone" (meaning my late governor--more tears)--"you don't, you cannot fancy that your own mother, who bore you, and nursed you, and wept for you, and would give her all to save you from a moment's harm--you don't suppose that she would che-e-e-eat you!" And here she gave a louder screech than ever, and flung back on the sofa; and one of my sisters went and tumbled into her arms, and t'other went round, and the kissing and slobbering scene went on again, only I was left out, thank goodness. I hate such sentimentality.

"CHE-E-E-EAT ME," says I, mocking her. "What do you mean, then, by saying you're so rich? Say, have you got money, or have you not?" (And I rapped out a good number of oaths, too, which I don't put in here; but I was in a dreadful fury, that's the fact.)

"So help me heaven," says mamma, in answer, going down on her knees and smacking her two hands, "I have but a Queen Anne's guinea in the whole of this wicked world."

"Then what, Madam, induces you to tell these absurd stories to me, and to talk about your riches, when you know that you and your daughters are beggars, Ma'am--BEGGARS?"

"My dearest boy, have we not got the house, and the furniture, and a hundred a year still; and have you not great talents, which will make all our fortunes?" says Mrs. Stubbs, getting up off her knees, and making believe to smile as she clawed hold of my hand and kissed it.

This was TOO cool. "YOU have got a hundred a year, Ma'am," says I--"YOU have got a house? Upon my soul and honor this is the first I ever heard of it; and I'll tell you what, Ma'am," says I (and it cut her PRETTY SHARPLY too): "as you've got it, YOU'D BETTER GO AND LIVE IN IT. I've got quite enough to do with my own house, and every penny of my own income."

Upon this speech the old lady said nothing, but she gave a screech loud enough to be heard from here to York, and down she fell--kicking and struggling in a regular fit.

*****

I did not see Mrs. Stubbs for some days after this, and the girls used to come down to meals, and never speak; going up again and stopping with their mother. At last, one day, both of them came in very solemn to my study, and Eliza, the eldest, said, "Robert, mamma has paid you our board up to Michaelmas."

"She has," says I; for I always took precious good care to have it in advance.

"She says, Robert, That on Michaelmas day--we'll--we'll go away, Robert."

"Oh, she's going to her own house, is she, Lizzy? Very good. She'll want the furniture, I suppose, and that she may have too, for I'm going to sell the place myself." And so THAT matter was settled.

*****

On Michaelmas day--and during these two months I hadn't, I do believe, seen my mother twice (once, about two o'clock in the morning, I woke and found her sobbing over my bed)--on Michaelmas-day morning, Eliza comes to me and says, "ROBERT, THEY WILL COME AND FETCH US AT SIX THIS EVENING." Well, as this was the last day, I went and got the best goose I could find (I don't think I ever saw a primer, or ate more hearty myself), and had it roasted at three, with a good pudding afterwards; and a glorious bowl of punch. "Here's a health to you, dear girls," says I, "and you, Ma, and good luck to all three; and as you've not eaten a morsel, I hope you won't object to a glass of punch. It's the old stuff, you know, Ma'am, that that Waters sent to my father fifteen years ago."

Six o'clock came, and with it came a fine barouche. As I live, Captain Waters was on the box (it was his coach); that old thief, Bates, jumped out, entered my house, and before I could say Jack Robinson, whipped off mamma to the carriage: the girls followed, just giving me a hasty shake of the hand; and as mamma was helped in, Mary Waters, who was sitting inside, flung her arms round her, and then round the girls; and the Doctor, who acted footman, jumped on the box, and off they went; taking no more notice of ME than if I'd been a nonentity.

Here's a picture of the whole business:--Mamma and Miss Waters are sitting kissing each other in the carriage, with the two girls in the back seat: Waters is driving (a precious bad driver he is too); and I'm standing at the garden door, and whistling. That old fool Mary Malowney is crying behind the garden gate: she went off next day along with the furniture; and I to get into that precious scrape which I shall mention next.

SEPTEMBER.--PLUCKING A GOOSE.

After my papa's death, as he left me no money, and only a little land, I put my estate into an auctioneer's hands, and determined to amuse my solitude with a trip to some of our fashionable watering-places. My house was now a desert to me. I need not say how the departure of my dear parent, and her children, left me sad and lonely.

Well, I had a little ready money, and, for the estate, expected a couple of thousand pounds. I had a good military-looking person: for though I had absolutely cut the old North Bungays (indeed, after my affair with Waters, Colonel Craw hinted to me, in the most friendly manner, that I had better resign)--though I had left the army, I still retained the rank of Captain; knowing the advantages attendant upon that title in a watering-place tour.

Captain Stubbs became a great dandy at Cheltenham, Harrogate, Bath, Leamington, and other places. I was a good whist and billiard player; so much so, that in many of these towns, the people used to refuse, at last, to play with me, knowing how far I was their superior. Fancy my surprise, about five years after the Portsmouth affair, when strolling one day up the High Street, in Leamington, my eyes lighted upon a young man, whom I remembered in a certain butcher's yard, and elsewhere--no other, in fact, than Dobble. He, too, was dressed en militaire, with a frogged coat and spurs; and was walking with a showy-looking, Jewish-faced, black-haired lady, glittering with chains and rings, with a green bonnet and a bird-of-Paradise--a lilac shawl, a yellow gown, pink silk stockings, and light-blue shoes. Three children, and a handsome footman, were walking behind her, and the party, not seeing me, entered the "Royal Hotel" together.

I was known myself at the "Royal," and calling one of the waiters, learned the names of the lady and gentleman. He was Captain Dobble, the son of the rich army-clothier, Dobble (Dobble, Hobble and Co. of Pall Mall);--the lady was a Mrs. Manasseh, widow of an American Jew, living quietly at Leamington with her children, but possessed of an immense property. There's no use to give one's self out to be an absolute pauper: so the fact is, that I myself went everywhere with the character of a man of very large means. My father had died, leaving me immense sums of money, and landed estates. Ah! I was the gentleman then, the real gentleman, and everybody was too happy to have me at table.

Well, I came the next day, and left a card for Dobble, with a note. He neither returned my visit, nor answered my note. The day after, however, I met him with the widow, as before; and going up to him, very kindly seized him by the hand, and swore I was--as really was the case--charmed to see him. Dobble hung back, to my surprise, and I do believe the creature would have cut me, if he dared; but I gave him a frown, and said--

"What, Dobble, my boy, don't you recollect old Stubbs, and our adventure with the butcher's daughters--ha?"

Dobble gave a sickly kind of grin, and said, "Oh! ah! yes! It is--yes! it is, I believe, Captain Stubbs."

"An old comrade, Madam, of Captain Dobble's, and one who has heard so much, and seen so much of your ladyship, that he must take the liberty of begging his friend to introduce him."

Dobble was obliged to take the hint; and Captain Stubbs was duly presented to Mrs. Manasseh. The lady was as gracious as possible; and when, at the end of the walk, we parted, she said "she hoped Captain Dobble would bring me to her apartments that evening, where she expected a few friends." Everybody, you see, knows everybody at Leamington; and I, for my part, was well known as a retired officer of the army, who, on his father's death, had come into seven thousand a year. Dobble's arrival had been subsequent to mine; but putting up as he did at the "Royal Hotel," and dining at the ordinary there with the widow, he had made her acquaintance before I had. I saw, however, that if I allowed him to talk about me, as he could, I should be compelled to give up all my hopes and pleasures at Leamington; and so I determined to be short with him. As soon as the lady had gone into the hotel, my friend Dobble was for leaving me likewise; but I stopped him and said, "Mr. Dobble, I saw what you meant just now: you wanted to cut me, because, forsooth, I did not choose to fight a duel at Portsmouth. Now look you, Dobble, I am no hero, but I'm not such a coward as you--and you know it. You are a very different man to deal with from Waters; and I WILL FIGHT this time."

Not perhaps that I would: but after the business of the butcher, I knew Dobble to be as great a coward as ever lived; and there never was any harm in threatening, for you know you are not obliged to stick to it afterwards. My words had their effect upon Dobble, who stuttered and looked red, and then declared he never had the slightest intention of passing me by; so we became friends, and his mouth was stopped.

He was very thick with the widow, but that lady had a very capacious heart, and there were a number of other gentlemen who seemed equally smitten with her. "Look at that Mrs. Manasseh," said a gentleman (it was droll, HE was a Jew, too) sitting at dinner by me. "She is old, and ugly, and yet, because she has money, all the men are flinging themselves at her."

"She has money, has she?"

"Eighty thousand pounds, and twenty thousand for each of her children. I know it FOR A FACT," said the strange gentleman. "I am in the law, and we of our faith, you know, know pretty well what the great families amongst us are worth."

"Who was Mr. Manasseh?" said I.

"A man of enormous wealth--a tobacco-merchant--West Indies; a fellow of no birth, however; and who, between ourselves, married a woman that is not much better than she should be. My dear sir," whispered he, "she is always in love. Now it is with that Captain Dobble; last week it was somebody else--and it may be you next week, if--ha! ha! ha!--you are disposed to enter the lists. I wouldn't, for MY part, have the woman with twice her money."

What did it matter to me whether the woman was good or not, provided she was rich? My course was quite clear. I told Dobble all that this gentleman had informed me, and being a pretty good hand at making a story, I made the widow appear SO bad, that the poor fellow was quite frightened, and fairly quitted the field. Ha! ha! I'm dashed if I did not make him believe that Mrs. Manasseh had MURDERED her last husband.

I played my game so well, thanks to the information that my friend the lawyer had given me, that in a month I had got the widow to show a most decided partial-

The Fatal Boots

ity for me. I sat by her at dinner, I drank with her at the "Wells"--I rode with her, I danced with her, and at a picnic to Kenilworth, where we drank a good deal of champagne, I actually popped the question, and was accepted. In another month, Robert Stubbs, Esq., led to the altar, Leah, widow of the late Z. Manasseh, Esq., of St. Kitt's!

*****

We drove up to London in her comfortable chariot: the children and servants following in a post-chaise. I paid, of course, for everything; and until our house in Berkeley Square was painted, we stopped at "Stevens's Hotel."

*****

My own estate had been sold, and the money was lying at a bank in the City. About three days after our arrival, as we took our breakfast in the hotel, previous to a visit to Mrs. Stubbs's banker, where certain little transfers were to be made, a gentleman was introduced, who, I saw at a glance, was of my wife's persuasion.

He looked at Mrs. Stubbs, and made a bow. "Perhaps it will be convenient to you to pay this little bill, one hundred and fifty-two pounds?"

"My love," says she, "will you pay this--it is a trifle which I had really forgotten?"

"My soul!" said I, "I have really not the money in the house."

"Vel, denn, Captain Shtubbsh," says he, "I must do my duty--and arrest you--here is the writ! Tom, keep the door?" My wife fainted--the children screamed, and I fancy my condition as I was obliged to march off to a spunging-house along with a horrid sheriff's officer?

OCTOBER.--MARS AND VENUS IN OPPOSITION.

I shall not describe my feelings when I found myself in a cage in Cursitor Street, instead of that fine house in Berkeley Square, which was to have been mine as the husband of Mrs. Manasseh. What a place!--in an odious, dismal street leading from Chancery Lane. A hideous Jew boy opened the second of three doors and shut it when Mr. Nabb and I (almost fainting) had entered; then he opened the third door, and then I was introduced to a filthy place called a coffee-room, which I exchanged for the solitary comfort of a little dingy back-parlor, where I was left for a while to brood over my miserable fate. Fancy the change between this and Berkeley Square! Was I, after all my pains, and cleverness, and perseverance, cheated at last? Had this Mrs. Manasseh been imposing upon me, and were the words of the wretch I met at the table-d'hote at Leamington only meant to mislead me and take me in? I determined to send for my wife, and know the whole truth. I saw at once that I had been the victim of an infernal plot, and that the carriage, the house in town, the West India fortune, were only so many lies which I had blindly believed. It was true that the debt was but a hundred and fifty pounds; and I had two thousand at my bankers'. But was the loss of HER 80,000L. nothing? Was the destruction of my hopes nothing? The accursed addition to my family of a Jewish wife and three Jewish children, nothing? And all these I was to support out of my two thousand pounds. I had better have stopped at home with my mamma and sisters, whom I really did love, and who produced me eighty pounds a year.

I had a furious interview with Mrs. Stubbs; and when I charged her, the base wretch! with cheating me, like a brazen serpent as she was, she flung back the cheat in my teeth, and swore I had swindled her. Why did I marry her, when she might have had twenty others? She only took me, she said, because I had twenty thousand pounds. I HAD said I possessed that sum; but in love, you know, and war all's fair.

The Fatal Boots

We parted quite as angrily as we met; and I cordially vowed that when I had paid the debt into which I had been swindled by her, I would take my 2,000L. and depart to some desert island; or, at the very least, to America, and never see her more, or any of her Israelitish brood. There was no use in remaining in the spunging-house (for I knew that there were such things as detainers, and that where Mrs. Stubbs owed a hundred pounds, she might owe a thousand) so I sent for Mr. Nabb, and tendering him a cheque for 150L. and his costs, requested to be let out forthwith. "Here, fellow," said I, "is a cheque on Child's for your paltry sum."

"It may be a sheck on Shild's," says Mr. Nabb; "but I should be a baby to let you out on such a paper as dat."

"Well," said I, "Child's is but a step from this: you may go and get the cash,--just give me an acknowledgment."

Nabb drew out the acknowledgment with great punctuality, and set off for the bankers', whilst I prepared myself for departure from this abominable prison.

He smiled as he came in. "Well," said I, "you have touched your money; and now, I must tell you, that you are the most infernal rogue and extortioner I ever met with."

"Oh, no, Mishter Shtubbsh," says he, grinning still. "Dere is som greater roag dan me,--mosh greater."

"Fellow," said I, "don't stand grinning before a gentleman; but give me my hat and cloak, and let me leave your filthy den."

"Shtop, Shtubbsh," says he, not even Mistering me this time. "Here ish a letter, vich you had better read."

I opened the letter; something fell to the ground:--it was my cheque.

The letter ran thus: "Messrs. Child and Co. present their compliments to Captain Stubbs, and regret that they have been obliged to refuse payment of the enclosed, having been served this day with an attachment by Messrs. Solomonson and Co., which compels them to retain Captain Stubbs' balance of 2,010L. 11s. 6d. until the decision of the suit of Solomonson v. Stubbs.

"FLEET STREET."

"You see," says Mr. Nabb, as I read this dreadful letter--"you see, Shtubbsh, dere vas two debts,--a little von and a big von. So dey arrested you for de little von, and attashed your money for de big von."

Don't laugh at me for telling this story. If you knew what tears are blotting over the paper as I write it--if you knew that for weeks after I was more like a madman than a sane man,--a madman in the Fleet Prison, where I went instead of to the desert island! What had I done to deserve it? Hadn't I always kept an eye to the main chance? Hadn't I lived economically, and not like other young men? Had I ever been known to squander or give away a single penny? No! I can lay my hand on my heart, and, thank heaven, say, No! Why, why was I punished so?

Let me conclude this miserable history. Seven months--my wife saw me once or twice, and then dropped me altogether--I remained in that fatal place. I wrote to my dear mamma, begging her to sell her furniture, but got no answer. All my old friends turned their backs upon me. My action went against me--I had not a penny to defend it. Solomonson proved my wife's debt, and seized my two thousand pounds. As for the detainer against me, I was obliged to go through the court for the relief of insolvent debtors. I passed through it, and came out a beggar. But fancy the malice of that wicked Stiffelkind: he appeared in court as my creditor for 3L., with sixteen years' interest at five per cent, for a PAIR OF TOP-BOOTS. The old thief produced them in court, and told the whole story--Lord Cornwallis, the detection, the pumping and all.

Commissioner Dubobwig was very funny about it. "So Doctor Swishtail would not pay you for the boots, eh, Mr. Stiffelkind?"

"No: he said, ven I asked him for payment, dey was ordered by a yong boy, and I ought to have gone to his schoolmaster."

"What! then you came on a BOOTLESS errand, ay, sir?" (A laugh.)

"Bootless! no sare, I brought de boots back vid me. How de devil else could I show dem to you?" (Another laugh.)

"You've never SOLED 'em since, Mr. Tickleshins?"

"I never would sell dem; I svore I never vood, on porpus to be revenged on dat Stobbs."

"What! your wound has never been HEALED, eh?"

"Vat do you mean vid your bootless errands, and your soling and healing? I tell you I have done vat I svore to do: I have exposed him at school; I have broak off a marriage for him, ven he vould have had twenty tousand pound; and now I have showed him up in a court of justice. Dat is vat I 'ave done, and dat's enough." And

The Fatal Boots

then the old wretch went down, whilst everybody was giggling and staring at poor me--as if I was not miserable enough already.

"This seems the dearest pair of boots you ever had in your life, Mr. Stubbs," said Commissioner Dubobwig very archly, and then he began to inquire about the rest of my misfortunes.

In the fulness of my heart I told him the whole of them: how Mr. Solomonson the attorney had introduced me to the rich widow, Mrs. Manasseh, who had fifty thousand pounds, and an estate in the West Indies. How I was married, and arrested on coming to town, and cast in an action for two thousand pounds brought against me by this very Solomonson for my wife's debts.

"Stop!" says a lawyer in the court. "Is this woman a showy black-haired woman with one eye? very often drunk, with three children?--Solomonson, short, with red hair?"

"Exactly so," said I, with tears in my eyes.

"That woman has married THREE MEN within the last two years. One in Ireland, and one at Bath. A Solomonson is, I believe, her husband, and they both are off for America ten days ago."

"But why did you not keep your 2,000L.?" said the lawyer.

"Sir, they attached it."

"Oh, well, we may pass you. You have been unlucky, Mr. Stubbs, but it seems as if the biter had been bit in this affair."

"No," said Mr. Dubobwig. "Mr. Stubbs is the victim of a FATAL ATTACHMENT."

NOVEMBER.--A GENERAL POST DELIVERY.

I was a free man when I went out of the Court; but I was a beggar--I, Captain Stubbs, of the bold North Bungays, did not know where I could get a bed, or a dinner.

As I was marching sadly down Portugal Street, I felt a hand on my shoulder and a rough voice which I knew well.

"Vell, Mr. Stobbs, have I not kept my promise? I told you dem boots would be your ruin."

I was much too miserable to reply; and only cast my eyes towards the roofs of the houses, which I could not see for the tears.

"Vat! you begin to gry and blobber like a shild? you vood marry, vood you? and noting vood do for you but a vife vid monny--ha, ha--but you vere de pigeon, and she was de grow. She has plocked you, too, pretty vell--eh? ha! ha!"

"Oh, Mr. Stiffelkind," said I, "don't laugh at my misery: she has not left me a single shilling under heaven. And I shall starve: I do believe I shall starve." And I began to cry fit to break my heart.

"Starf! stoff and nonsense! You vill never die of starfing--you vill die of HANGING, I tink--ho! ho!--and it is moch easier vay too." I didn't say a word, but cried on; till everybody in the street turned round and stared.

"Come, come," said Stiffelkind, "do not gry, Gaptain Stobbs--it is not goot for a Gaptain to gry--ha! ha! Dere--come vid me, and you shall have a dinner, and a bregfast too,--vich shall gost you noting, until you can bay vid your earnings."

And so this curious old man, who had persecuted me all through my prosperity, grew compassionate towards me in my ill-luck; and took me home with him as he promised. "I saw your name among de Insolvents, and I vowed, you know, to make you repent dem boots. Dere, now, it is done and forgotten, look you. Here,

Betty, Bettchen, make de spare bed, and put a clean knife and fork; Lort Cornvallis is come to dine vid me."

I lived with this strange old man for six weeks. I kept his books, and did what little I could to make myself useful: carrying about boots and shoes, as if I had never borne his Majesty's commission. He gave me no money, but he fed and lodged me comfortably. The men and boys used to laugh, and call me General, and Lord Cornwallis, and all sorts of nicknames; and old Stiffelkind made a thousand new ones for me.

One day I can recollect--one miserable day, as I was polishing on the trees a pair of boots of Mr. Stiffelkind's manufacture--the old gentleman came into the shop, with a lady on his arm.

"Vere is Gaptain Stobbs?" said he. "Vere is dat ornament to his Majesty's service?"

I came in from the back shop, where I was polishing the boots, with one of them in my hand.

"Look, my dear," says he, "here is an old friend of yours, his Excellency Lort Cornvallis!--Who would have thought such a nobleman vood turn shoeblack? Captain Stobbs, here is your former flame, my dear niece, Miss Grotty. How could you, Magdalen, ever leaf such a lof of a man? Shake hands vid her, Gaptain;--dere, never mind de blacking!" But Miss drew back.

"I never shake hands with a SHOEBLACK," said she, mighty contemptuous.

"Bah! my lof, his fingers von't soil you. Don't you know he has just been VITE-VASHED?"

"I wish, uncle," says she, "you would not leave me with such low people."

"Low, because he cleans boots? De Gaptain prefers PUMPS to boots I tink--ha! ha!"

"Captain indeed! a nice Captain," says Miss Crutty, snapping her fingers in my face, and walking away: "a Captain who has had his nose pulled! ha! ha!"--And how could I help it? it wasn't by my own CHOICE that that ruffian Waters took such liberties with me. Didn't I show how averse I was to all quarrels by refusing altogether his challenge?--But such is the world. And thus the people at Stiffelkind's used to tease me, until they drove me almost mad.

At last he came home one day more merry and abusive than ever. "Gaptain," says he, "I have goot news for you--a goot place. Your lordship vill not be able to geep your garridge, but you vill be gomfortable, and serve his Majesty."

"Serve his Majesty?" says I. "Dearest Mr. Stiffelkind, have you got me a place under Government?"

"Yes, and somting better still--not only a place, but a uniform: yes, Gaptain Stobbs, a RED GOAT."

"A red coat! I hope you don't think I would demean myself by entering the ranks of the army? I am a gentleman, Mr. Stiffelkind--I can never--no, I never--"

"No, I know you will never--you are too great a goward--ha! ha!--though dis is a red goat, and a place where you must give some HARD KNOCKS too--ha! ha!--do you gomprehend?--and you shall be a general instead of a gaptain--ha! ha!"

"A general in a red coat, Mr. Stiffelkind?"

"Yes, a GENERAL BOSTMAN!--ha! ha! I have been vid your old friend, Bunting, and he has an uncle in the Post Office, and he has got you de place--eighteen shillings a veek, you rogue, and your goat. You must not oben any of de letters you know."

And so it was--I, Robert Stubbs, Esquire, became the vile thing he named--a general postman!

*****

I was so disgusted with Stiffelkind's brutal jokes, which were now more brutal than ever, that when I got my place in the Post Office, I never went near the fellow again: for though he had done me a favor in keeping me from starvation, he certainly had done it in a very rude, disagreeable manner, and showed a low and mean spirit in SHOVING me into such a degraded place as that of postman. But what had I to do? I submitted to fate, and for three years or more, Robert Stubbs, of the North Bungay Fencibles, was--

I wonder nobody recognized me. I lived in daily fear the first year: but afterwards grew accustomed to my situation, as all great men will do, and wore my red coat as naturally as if I had been sent into the world only for the purpose of being a letter-carrier.

The Fatal Boots

I was first in the Whitechapel district, where I stayed for nearly three years, when I was transferred to Jermyn Street and Duke Street--famous places for lodgings. I suppose I left a hundred letters at a house in the latter street, where lived some people who must have recognized me had they but once chanced to look at me.

You see that when I left Sloffemsquiggle, and set out in the gay world, my mamma had written to me a dozen times at least; but I never answered her, for I knew she wanted money, and I detest writing. Well, she stopped her letters, finding she could get none from me:--but when I was in the Fleet, as I told you, I wrote repeatedly to my dear mamma, and was not a little nettled at her refusing to notice me in my distress, which is the very time one most wants notice.

Stubbs is not an uncommon name; and though I saw MRS. STUBBS on a little bright brass plate, in Duke street, and delivered so many letters to the lodgers in her house, I never thought of asking who she was, or whether she was my relation, or not.

One day the young woman who took in the letters had not got change, and she called her mistress. An old lady in a poke-bonnet came out of the parlor, and put on her spectacles, and looked at the letter, and fumbled in her pocket for eightpence, and apologized to the postman for keeping him waiting. And when I said, "Never mind, Ma'am, it's no trouble," the old lady gave a start, and then she pulled off her spectacles, and staggered back; and then she began muttering, as if about to choke; and then she gave a great screech, and flung herself into my arms, and roared out, "MY SON, MY SON!"

"Law, mamma," said I, "is that you?" and I sat down on the hall bench with her, and let her kiss me as much as ever she liked. Hearing the whining and crying, down comes another lady from up stairs,--it was my sister Eliza; and down come the lodgers. And the maid gets water and what not, and I was the regular hero of the group. I could not stay long then, having my letters to deliver. But, in the evening, after mail-time, I went back to my mamma and sister; and, over a bottle of prime old port, and a precious good leg of boiled mutton and turnips, made myself pretty comfortable, I can tell you.

DECEMBER.--"THE WINTER OF OUR DISCONTENT."

Mamma had kept the house in Duke Street for more than two years. I recollected some of the chairs and tables from dear old Sloffemsquiggle, and the bowl in which I had made that famous rum-punch, the evening she went away, which she and my sisters left untouched, and I was obliged to drink after they were gone; but that's not to the purpose.

Think of my sister Lucy's luck! that chap, Waters, fell in love with her, and married her; and she now keeps her carriage, and lives in state near Sloffemsquiggle. I offered to make it up with Waters; but he bears malice, and never will see or speak to me.--He had the impudence, too, to say, that he took in all letters for mamma at Sloffemsquiggle; and that as mine were all begging-letters, he burned them, and never said a word to her concerning them. He allowed mamma fifty pounds a year, and, if she were not such a fool, she might have had three times as much; but the old lady was high and mighty forsooth, and would not be beholden, even to her own daughter, for more than she actually wanted. Even this fifty pound she was going to refuse; but when I came to live with her, of course I wanted pocket-money as well as board and lodging, and so I had the fifty pounds for MY share, and eked out with it as well as I could.

Old Bates and the Captain, between them, gave mamma a hundred pounds when she left me (she had the deuce's own luck, to be sure--much more than ever fell to ME, I know) and as she said she WOULD try and work for her living, it was thought best to take a house and let lodgings, which she did. Our first and second floor paid us four guineas a week, on an average; and the front parlor and attic made forty pounds more. Mamma and Eliza used to have the front attic: but I took that, and they slept in the servants' bedroom. Lizzy had a pretty genius for work, and earned a guinea a week that way; so that we had got nearly two hundred a year over the rent to keep house with,--and we got on pretty well. Besides, women eat nothing: my women didn't care for meat for days together sometimes,--so that it was only necessary to dress a good steak or so for me.

Mamma would not think of my continuing in the Post Office. She said her dear Robert, her husband's son, her gallant soldier, and all that, should remain at home and be a gentleman--which I was, certainly, though I didn't find fifty pounds a year very much to buy clothes and be a gentleman upon. To be sure, mother found me shirts and linen, so that THAT wasn't in the fifty pounds. She kicked a little at paying the washing too; but she gave in at last, for I was her dear Bob, you know; and I'm blest if I could not make her give me the gown off her back. Fancy! once she cut up a very nice rich black silk scarf, which my sister Waters sent her, and made me a waistcoat and two stocks of it. She was so VERY soft, the old lady!

*****

I'd lived in this way for five years or more, making myself content with my fifty pounds a year (PERHAPS I had saved a little out of it; but that's neither here nor there). From year's end to year's end I remained faithful to my dear mamma, never leaving her except for a month or so in the summer--when a bachelor may take a trip to Gravesend or Margate, which would be too expensive for a family. I say a bachelor, for the fact is, I don't know whether I am married or not--never having heard a word since of the scoundrelly Mrs. Stubbs.

I never went to the public-house before meals: for, with my beggarly fifty pounds, I could not afford to dine away from home: but there I had my regular seat, and used to come home PRETTY GLORIOUS, I can tell you. Then bed till eleven; then breakfast and the newspaper; then a stroll in Hyde Park or St. James's; then home at half-past three to dinner--when I jollied, as I call it, for the rest of the day. I was my mother's delight; and thus, with a clear conscience, I managed to live on.

*****

How fond she was of me, to be sure! Being sociable myself, and loving to have my friends about me, we often used to assemble a company of as hearty fellows as you would wish to sit down with, and keep the nights up royally. "Never mind, my boys," I used to say. "Send the bottle round: mammy pays for all." As she did, sure enough: and sure enough we punished her cellar too. The good old lady used to wait upon us, as if for all the world she had been my servant, instead of a lady and my mamma. Never used she to repine, though I often, as I must confess, gave her occasion (keeping her up till four o'clock in the morning, because she never could sleep until she saw her "dear Bob" in bed, and leading her a sad anxious life). She was of such a sweet temper, the old lady, that I think in the course of five years I never knew her in a passion, except twice: and then with sister Lizzy, who declared I was ruining the house, and driving the lodgers away, one by one. But mamma would not hear of such envious spite on my sister's part. "Her Bob" was always right, she said. At last Lizzy fairly retreated, and went to the Waters's.--I was glad of it, for her temper was dreadful, and we used to be squabbling from morning till night!

Ah, those WERE jolly times! but Ma was obliged to give up the lodging-house at last--for, somehow, things went wrong after my sister's departure--the nasty uncharitable people said, on account of ME; because I drove away the lodgers by smoking and drinking, and kicking up noises in the house; and because Ma gave me so much of her money:--so she did, but if she WOULD give it, you know, how could I help it? Heigho! I wish I'd KEPT it.

No such luck. The business I thought was to last for ever: but at the end of two years came a smash--shut up shop--sell off everything. Mamma went to the Waters's: and, will you believe it? the ungrateful wretches would not receive me! that Mary, you see, was SO disappointed at not marrying me. Twenty pounds a year they allow, it is true; but what's that for a gentleman? For twenty years I have been struggling manfully to gain an honest livelihood, and, in the course of them, have seen a deal of life, to be sure. I've sold cigars and pocket-handkerchiefs at the corners of streets; I've been a billiard-marker; I've been a director (in the panic year) of the Imperial British Consolidated Mangle and Drying Ground Company. I've been on the stage (for two years as an actor, and about a month as a cad, when I was very low); I've been the means of giving to the police of this empire some very valuable information (about licensed victuallers, gentlemen's carts, and pawnbrokers' names); I've been very nearly an officer again--that is, an assistant to an officer of the Sheriff of Middlesex: it was my last place.

On the last day of the year 1837, even THAT game was up. It's a thing that very seldom happened to a gentleman, to be kicked out of a spunging-house; but such was my case. Young Nabb (who succeeded his father) drove me ignominiously from his door, because I had charged a gentleman in the coffee-rooms seven-and-sixpence for a glass of ale and bread and cheese, the charge of the house being only six shillings. He had the meanness to deduct the eighteenpence from my wages, and because I blustered a bit, he took me by the shoulders and turned me out--me, a gentleman, and, what is more, a poor orphan!

How I did rage and swear at him when I got out into the street! There stood he, the hideous Jew monster, at the double door, writhing under the effect of my language. I had my revenge! Heads were thrust out of every bar of his windows, laughing at him. A crowd gathered round me, as I stood pounding him with my satire, and they evidently enjoyed his discomfiture. I think the mob would have pelted the ruffian to death (one or two of their missiles hit ME, I can tell you), when a policeman came up, and in reply to a gentleman, who was asking what was the disturbance, said, "Bless you, sir, it's Lord Cornwallis." "Move on, BOOTS," said the fellow to me; for the fact is, my misfortunes and early life are pretty well known-- and so the crowd dispersed.

"What could have made that policeman call you Lord Cornwallis and Boots?" said the gentleman, who seemed mightily amused, and had followed me. "Sir," says I, "I am an unfortunate officer of the North Bungay Fencibles, and I'll tell you willingly for a pint of beer." He told me to follow him to his chambers in the Temple, which I did (a five-pair back), and there, sure enough, I had the beer; and told him this very story you've been reading. You see he is what is called a literary man--and sold my adventures for me to the booksellers; he's a strange chap; and says they're MORAL.

*****

I'm blest if I can see anything moral in them. I'm sure I ought to have been more lucky through life, being so very wide awake. And yet here I am, without a place, or even a friend, starving upon a beggarly twenty pounds a year--not a single sixpence more, upon MY HONOR.

www.bookjungle.com email: sales@bookjungle.com fax: 630-214-0564 mail: Book Jungle PO Box 2226 Champaign, IL 61825

The Codes Of Hammurabi And Moses
W. W. Davies

QTY

The discovery of the Hammurabi Code is one of the greatest achievements of archaeology, and is of paramount interest, not only to the student of the Bible, but also to all those interested in ancient history...

Religion   ISBN: *1-59462-338-4*   Pages:132
                                                MSRP $12.95

The Theory of Moral Sentiments
Adam Smith

QTY

This work from 1749. contains original theories of conscience amd moral judgment and it is the foundation for systemof morals.

Philosophy ISBN: *1-59462-777-0*   Pages:536
                                                MSRP $19.95

Jessica's First Prayer
Hesba Stretton

QTY

In a screened and secluded corner of one of the many railway-bridges which span the streets of London there could be seen a few years ago, from five o'clock every morning until half past eight, a tidily set-out coffee-stall, consisting of a trestle and board, upon which stood two large tin cans, with a small fire of charcoal burning under each so as to keep the coffee boiling during the early hours of the morning when the work-people were thronging into the city on their way to their daily toil...

Childrens   ISBN: *1-59462-373-2*   Pages:84
                                                MSRP $9.95

My Life and Work
Henry Ford

QTY

Henry Ford revolutionized the world with his implementation of mass production for the Model T automobile. Gain valuable business insight into his life and work with his own auto-biography... "We have only started on our development of our country we have not as yet, with all our talk of wonderful progress, done more than scratch the surface. The progress has been wonderful enough but..."

Biographies/ ISBN: *1-59462-198-5*   Pages:300
                                                MSRP $21.95

www.bookjungle.com *email: sales@bookjungle.com fax: 630-214-0564 mail: Book Jungle PO Box 2226 Champaign, IL 61825*

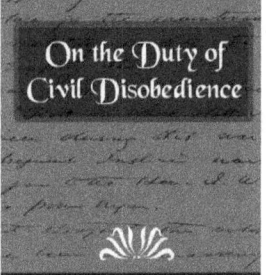

The Art of Cross-Examination
Francis Wellman

QTY

I presume it is the experience of every author, after his first book is published upon an important subject, to be almost overwhelmed with a wealth of ideas and illustrations which could readily have been included in his book, and which to his own mind, at least, seem to make a second edition inevitable. Such certainly was the case with me; and when the first edition had reached its sixth impression in five months, I rejoiced to learn that it seemed to my publishers that the book had met with a sufficiently favorable reception to justify a second and considerably enlarged edition. ..

Reference   ISBN: *1-59462-647-2*

Pages:412
MSRP $19.95

On the Duty of Civil Disobedience
Henry David Thoreau

QTY

Thoreau wrote his famous essay, On the Duty of Civil Disobedience, as a protest against an unjust but popular war and the immoral but popular institution of slave-owning. He did more than write—he declined to pay his taxes, and was hauled off to gaol in consequence. Who can say how much this refusal of his hastened the end of the war and of slavery ?

Law   ISBN: *1-59462-747-9*

Pages:48
MSRP $7.45

Dream Psychology Psychoanalysis for Beginners
Sigmund Freud

QTY

Sigmund Freud, born Sigismund Schlomo Freud (May 6, 1856 - September 23, 1939), was a Jewish-Austrian neurologist and psychiatrist who co-founded the psychoanalytic school of psychology. Freud is best known for his theories of the unconscious mind, especially involving the mechanism of repression; his redefinition of sexual desire as mobile and directed towards a wide variety of objects; and his therapeutic techniques, especially his understanding of transference in the therapeutic relationship and the presumed value of dreams as sources of insight into unconscious desires.

Psychology   ISBN: *1-59462-905-6*

Pages:196
MSRP $15.45

The Miracle of Right Thought
Orison Swett Marden

QTY

Believe with all of your heart that you will do what you were made to do. When the mind has once formed the habit of holding cheerful, happy, prosperous pictures, it will not be easy to form the opposite habit. It does not matter how improbable or how far away this realization may see, or how dark the prospects may be, if we visualize them as best we can, as vividly as possible, hold tenaciously to them and vigorously struggle to attain them, they will gradually become actualized, realized in the life. But a desire, a longing without endeavor, a yearning abandoned or held indifferently will vanish without realization.

Self Help   ISBN: *1-59462-644-8*

Pages:360
MSRP $25.45

www.bookjungle.com email: sales@bookjungle.com fax: 630-214-0564 mail: Book Jungle PO Box 2226 Champaign, IL 61825

QTY

- [ ] **The Rosicrucian Cosmo-Conception Mystic Christianity** by *Max Heindel* ISBN: *1-59462-188-8* **$38.95**
  The Rosicrucian Cosmo-conception is not dogmatic, neither does it appeal to any other authority than the reason of the student. It is: not controversial, but is: sent forth in the, hope that it may help to clear... New Age/Religion Pages 646

- [ ] **Abandonment To Divine Providence** by *Jean-Pierre de Caussade* ISBN: *1-59462-228-0* **$25.95**
  "The Rev. Jean Pierre de Caussade was one of the most remarkable spiritual writers of the Society of Jesus in France in the 18th Century. His death took place at Toulouse in 1751. His works have gone through many editions and have been republished... Inspirational/Religion Pages 400

- [ ] **Mental Chemistry** by *Charles Haanel* ISBN: *1-59462-192-6* **$23.95**
  Mental Chemistry allows the change of material conditions by combining and appropriately utilizing the power of the mind. Much like applied chemistry creates something new and unique out of careful combinations of chemicals the mastery of mental chemistry... New Age Pages 354

- [ ] **The Letters of Robert Browning and Elizabeth Barret Barrett 1845-1846 vol II** ISBN: *1-59462-193-4* **$35.95**
  by *Robert Browning* and *Elizabeth Barrett*
  Biographies Pages 596

- [ ] **Gleanings In Genesis (volume I)** by *Arthur W. Pink* ISBN: *1-59462-130-6* **$27.45**
  Appropriately has Genesis been termed "the seed plot of the Bible" for in it we have, in germ form, almost all of the great doctrines which are afterwards fully developed in the books of Scripture which follow... Religion/Inspirational Pages 420

- [ ] **The Master Key** by *L. W. de Laurence* ISBN: *1-59462-001-6* **$30.95**
  In no branch of human knowledge has there been a more lively increase of the spirit of research during the past few years than in the study of Psychology, Concentration and Mental Discipline. The requests for authentic lessons in Thought Control, Mental Discipline and... New Age/Business Pages 422

- [ ] **The Lesser Key Of Solomon Goetia** by *L. W. de Laurence* ISBN: *1-59462-092-X* **$9.95**
  This translation of the first book of the "Lernegton" which is now for the first time made accessible to students of Talismanic Magic was done, after careful collation and edition, from numerous Ancient Manuscripts in Hebrew, Latin, and French... New Age/Occult Pages 92

- [ ] **Rubaiyat Of Omar Khayyam** by *Edward Fitzgerald* ISBN: *1-59462-332-5* **$13.95**
  Edward Fitzgerald, whom the world has already learned, in spite of his own efforts to remain within the shadow of anonymity, to look upon as one of the rarest poets of the century, was born at Bredfield, in Suffolk, on the 31st of March, 1809. He was the third son of John Purcell... Music Pages 172

- [ ] **Ancient Law** by *Henry Maine* ISBN: *1-59462-128-4* **$29.95**
  The chief object of the following pages is to indicate some of the earliest ideas of mankind, as they are reflected in Ancient Law, and to point out the relation of those ideas to modern thought. Religion/History Pages 452

- [ ] **Far-Away Stories** by *William J. Locke* ISBN: *1-59462-129-2* **$19.45**
  "Good wine needs no bush, but a collection of mixed vintages does. And this book is just such a collection. Some of the stories I do not want to remain buried for ever in the museum files of dead magazine-numbers an author's not unpardonable vanity..." Fiction Pages 272

- [ ] **Life of David Crockett** by *David Crockett* ISBN: *1-59462-250-7* **$27.45**
  "Colonel David Crockett was one of the most remarkable men of the times in which he lived. Born in humble life, but gifted with a strong will, an indomitable courage, and unremitting perseverance... Biographies/New Age Pages 424

- [ ] **Lip-Reading** by *Edward Nitchie* ISBN: *1-59462-206-X* **$25.95**
  Edward B. Nitchie, founder of the New York School for the Hard of Hearing, now the Nitchie School of Lip-Reading, Inc, wrote "LIP-READING Principles and Practice". The development and perfecting of this meritorious work on lip-reading was an undertaking... How-to Pages 400

- [ ] **A Handbook of Suggestive Therapeutics, Applied Hypnotism, Psychic Science** ISBN: *1-59462-214-0* **$24.95**
  by *Henry Munro*
  Health/New Age/Health/Self-help Pages 376

- [ ] **A Doll's House: and Two Other Plays** by *Henrik Ibsen* ISBN: *1-59462-112-8* **$19.95**
  Henrik Ibsen created this classic when in revolutionary 1848 Rome. Introducing some striking concepts in playwriting for the realist genre, this play has been studied the world over. Fiction/Classics/Plays 308

- [ ] **The Light of Asia** by *sir Edwin Arnold* ISBN: *1-59462-204-3* **$13.95**
  In this poetic masterpiece, Edwin Arnold describes the life and teachings of Buddha. The man who was to become known as Buddha to the world was born as Prince Gautama of India but he rejected the worldly riches and abandoned the reigns of power when... Religion/History/Biographies Pages 170

- [ ] **The Complete Works of Guy de Maupassant** by *Guy de Maupassant* ISBN: *1-59462-157-8* **$16.95**
  "For days and days, nights and nights, I had dreamed of that first kiss which was to consecrate our engagement, and I knew not on what spot I should put my lips..." Fiction/Classics Pages 240

- [ ] **The Art of Cross-Examination** by *Francis L. Wellman* ISBN: *1-59462-309-0* **$26.95**
  Written by a renowned trial lawyer, Wellman imparts his experience and uses case studies to explain how to use psychology to extract desired information through questioning. How-to/Science/Reference Pages 408

- [ ] **Answered or Unanswered?** by *Louisa Vaughan* ISBN: *1-59462-248-5* **$10.95**
  Miracles of Faith in China
  Religion Pages 112

- [ ] **The Edinburgh Lectures on Mental Science (1909)** by *Thomas* ISBN: *1-59462-008-3* **$11.95**
  This book contains the substance of a course of lectures recently given by the writer in the Queen Street Hall, Edinburgh. Its purpose is to indicate the Natural Principles governing the relation between Mental Action and Material Conditions... New Age/Psychology Pages 148

- [ ] **Ayesha** by *H. Rider Haggard* ISBN: *1-59462-301-5* **$24.95**
  Verily and indeed it is the unexpected that happens! Probably if there was one person upon the earth from whom the Editor of this, and of a certain previous history, did not expect to hear again... Classics Pages 380

- [ ] **Ayala's Angel** by *Anthony Trollope* ISBN: *1-59462-352-X* **$29.95**
  The two girls were both pretty, but Lucy who was twenty-one who supposed to be simple and comparatively unattractive, whereas Ayala was credited, as her Bombwhat romantic name might show, with poetic charm and a taste for romance. Ayala when her father died was nineteen... Fiction Pages 484

- [ ] **The American Commonwealth** by *James Bryce* ISBN: *1-59462-286-8* **$34.45**
  An interpretation of American democratic political theory. It examines political mechanics and society from the perspective of Scotsman James Bryce. Politics Pages 572

- [ ] **Stories of the Pilgrims** by *Margaret P. Pumphrey* ISBN: *1-59462-116-0* **$17.95**
  This book explores pilgrims religious oppression in England as well as their escape to Holland and eventual crossing to America on the Mayflower, and their early days in New England... History Pages 268

www.bookjungle.com *email:* sales@bookjungle.com *fax:* 630-214-0564 *mail:* Book Jungle PO Box 2226 Champaign, IL 61825

			QTY
The Fasting Cure by **Sinclair Upton**	ISBN: *1-59462-222-1*	**$13.95**	☐
In the Cosmopolitan Magazine for May, 1910, and in the Contemporary Review (London) for April, 1910, I published an article dealing with my experiences in fasting. I have written a great many magazine articles, but never one which attracted so much attention...		*New Age/Self Help/Health Pages 164*	
Hebrew Astrology by **Sepharial**	ISBN: *1-59462-308-2*	**$13.45**	☐
In these days of advanced thinking it is a matter of common observation that we have left many of the old landmarks behind and that we are now pressing forward to greater heights and to a wider horizon than that which represented the mind-content of our progenitors...		*Astrology Pages 144*	
Thought Vibration or The Law of Attraction in the Thought World	ISBN: *1-59462-127-6*	**$12.95**	☐
by **William Walker Atkinson**		*Psychology/Religion Pages 144*	
Optimism by **Helen Keller**	ISBN: *1-59462-108-X*	**$15.95**	☐
Helen Keller was blind, deaf, and mute since 19 months old, yet famously learned how to overcome these handicaps, communicate with the world, and spread her lectures promoting optimism. An inspiring read for everyone...		*Biographies/Inspirational Pages 84*	
Sara Crewe by **Frances Burnett**	ISBN: *1-59462-360-0*	**$9.45**	☐
In the first place, Miss Minchin lived in London. Her home was a large, dull, tall one, in a large, dull square, where all the houses were alike, and all the sparrows were alike, and where all the door-knockers made the same heavy sound...		*Childrens/Classic Pages 88*	
The Autobiography of Benjamin Franklin by **Benjamin Franklin**	ISBN: *1-59462-135-7*	**$24.95**	☐
The Autobiography of Benjamin Franklin has probably been more extensively read than any other American historical work, and no other book of its kind has had such ups and downs of fortune. Franklin lived for many years in England, where he was agent...		*Biographies/History Pages 332*	

Name	
Email	
Telephone	
Address	
City, State ZIP	

☐ Credit Card   ☐ Check / Money Order

Credit Card Number	
Expiration Date	
Signature	

Please Mail to: Book Jungle
PO Box 2226
Champaign, IL 61825
or Fax to: 630-214-0564

ORDERING INFORMATION
web: *www.bookjungle.com*
email: *sales@bookjungle.com*
fax: *630-214-0564*
mail: *Book Jungle PO Box 2226 Champaign, IL 61825*
or PayPal *to sales@bookjungle.com*

Please contact us for bulk discounts

DIRECT-ORDER TERMS

**20% Discount if You Order
Two or More Books**
Free Domestic Shipping!
Accepted: Master Card, Visa,
Discover, American Express

www.ingramcontent.com/pod-product-compliance
Lightning Source LLC
Chambersburg PA
CBHW081329040426
42453CB00013B/2349